Nils Klippstein

A Course in Love & Miracles

This Is a Growing Book

Nils is an intuitive author, heart chakra coach and dark retreat shaman. His work includes heart opening, yin-yang balance, shadow work, kundalini, angelic humans, fasting and breatharian lifestyle, connection with our spirit guides, energetic healing of the astral and emotional body, hugging meditations, sacred sensuality, forgiveness work ... as well as opening relationships in a safe, balanced and stable way through individual allowances and boundaries within a relationship network.

In his work he explores and describes the higher dimensions, the sacred trinity (feminine, masculine and the union of both) and is committed to having Gaia (Mother Earth) and the other stars and planets recognised as highly evolved, higher conscious beings.

www.sensual-energetic-healing.com
www.healer-and-creator.de/en
www.nils-klippstein.de/en

Thank you, Goddess Gaia.

You have gifted us with a whole personal universe

to explore, grow, and heal.

Through your divine guidance,

our shadow work and forgiving,

we can become healers and creators.

And when the body becomes too small to hold us,

we can grow further

and become a celestial being just like you.

Contents

You Only Pay for Printing ...

... because the systems of the old world for selling my books have failed me. Publishers and social media platforms don't spread my work enough to make a living from it.

After trying many ways to "get out there", I realised that this new world must be based on open, honest sharing without expectations. This brings me into full trust that my personal universe (lovingly guided by Gaia) will always take good care of me.

Since many things still cost money, I cannot live for free. As the new world is not yet fully born, I still pay for food and water, internet and software, travel and events, ... like everyone else.

Would you like to give back?

Perhaps you choose something from this list of suggestions, or come up with something else:

- You could become a Patron and support me with a monthly donation:
  https://www.patreon.com/nilsklippstein

- You could "buy me a coffee":
  https://buymeacoffee.com/nilsklippstein

- You could donate via PayPal:
  https://paypal.me/NilsKlippstein
  (nils@start2dream.de).

- You could ask me to do a live reading, online or offline, and make a donation.

- You could visit me for a shared time together, let me guide and support you in any of my topics (see: page two) and make a donation.

- You could give this book to nine (or more) of your friends, acquaintances and colleagues and ask them to support me if they can.

Thank you for your consideration.

Let LOVE be thy medicine!

Foreword

Greetings, I am Nils, intuitive author and creator of this course for more self-love. Welcome, dear heartfelt soul, to the magical world of Sanuela. Thank you for joining me on this journey!

By reading spiritual books, we can fall into the mental trap of consumption without much progress in our growth or inner healing. I am very familiar with this mistake from my own past. This course accompanies my book *High Priestess of Sanuela*, so that you will have the chance to apply its content to your life.

If you haven't read the book yet, it isn't a problem - just follow along with the short excerpts contained in this course. Later, when the time is right for you, perhaps you will want to read my "spiritual fantasy romance".

Allow me to introduce myself shortly. From a young age, I was interested in spirituality. I left school early to spend three years in a meditation-focused community. Later, I experienced the highs and lows of a party lifestyle and the business world.

Eventually, I found my way back to my inner heart centre through shamanic ceremonies and self-love retreats on the beautiful island of Tenerife. connecting with my spirit guides who now guide me in my writing and my life.

I wish you many loving experiences and miracles throughout this course! If you wish to contact me personally, please find my contact details on the "About Me" page on my website

https://www.sensual-energetic-healing.com

Love and peace,

Nils

How This Course Works

This course follows the story of Ayana and offers daily ideas to reflect on and implement in a comfortable way.

All exercises are suggestions, so have fun and be imaginative. Trust your intuition and adapt it to your personal growth journey.

I strongly suggest that you keep a journal of love and miracles while you are taking the course.

The writing will help you to better process all your emotions and feelings about love and your relationships with others. Please write in your journal even if it's not mentioned in the exercise description.

The course can be done daily but you can take a break if you're busy. Find your own pace, but please take 24 hours for each step and reflect, breathe consciously, and journal your experiences, what you feel, and what comes up within.

So far, the course contains exercises for 33 days, reaching to the beginning of chapter three in *High*

Priestess of Sanuela. If you would like to help this book to grow, I would ask you to look again at the chapter *You Only Pay for Printing*.

When I see a certain flow of interest and support, I wish to continue writing on the course. If you have received the Kindle version on Amazon, you will receive all updates automatically. If you found the book through friends or on the internet, you will need to check on my website if an update is available and download it manually.

Are you ready to start your self-love journey with Ayana?

Day 1: Experiencing Miracles & Heart Chakra Breathing

When we open our hearts wider and wider, we can expect miracles to occur in our lives. We might notice more double numbers and synchronicities. Things in our life will seemingly "coincidentally" or automatically fall in place more and more.

This doesn't always mean that everything will be easy. By honestly opening up more to ourselves, to our self-love and our path back to our inner centre, we will need to go through all the necessary inner processing. In doing so, we create what we have to learn along the way.

Have you heard of the Heart Chakra Breathing exercise? I call it the perhaps simplest spiritual exercise of them all. You imagine breathing through your heart chakra. That is all. Inhale love, exhale love.

Please give it a try and bring more love into your life from today onwards. The highest art is to keep going and to start the Heart Chakra Breathing again and again, whenever you think of it.

The more often we focus our attention on our heart, the more often miracles can occur.

If you like, write some notes in your journal of love and miracles how you felt after breathing through your inner heart centre.

Please dedicate a full 24 hours to practicing your Heart Chakra Breathing as often as you wish. Tomorrow, when you are ready to continue, read the next chapter. Thank you.

Sending you lots of love and see you tomorrow!

Day 2: A Mindful Stroll

Please read the following first three paragraphs of *High Priestess of Sanuela* and imagine yourself as Ayana taking this stroll in the morning. Notice how attentive she is to the surrounding beauty…

…

A young woman wandered through a sunlit meadow, humming softly to herself, her heart feeling lighter than it had in a long time. The early spring air was fresh and fragrant, and the colourful flowers that lined the path seemed to draw her forward. She breathed in deeply, savouring the scent of the daisies, the roses, and the newly bloomed violets.

Ayana turned around and looked with a sense of familiarity and pride at her home village, from the huts made of straw and mud bricks, to the laughter of children playing in the narrow dirt streets. The people of Luminae, a mixture of cultures, appeared to Ayana like a patchwork quilt of her past, present, and future. This village had seen her through every joy and hardship.

Ayana took a deep breath, taking in the salty morning air. She could feel the cool breeze on her skin as she moved closer to the coast. The sun was shining brightly, reflecting off the water's surface. She watched the crashing waves build up small puddles of water on the sand beneath her, creating a serene and calming sound.

…

Why not take a brief mindful walk, even if it's only for five or ten minutes? It doesn't matter whether you live in a beautiful natural surrounding or in a noisy town: Find the beauty in tree and plant beings, children, birds, a beautiful picture, or interesting patterns.

While you walk, breathe through your heart chakra. Acknowledge the beauty. Perhaps, you want to express gratitude to all the beings and everything that you see for being part of your life experience?

Later, would you like to write down everything you were grateful for in your journal?

Much love, and until tomorrow!

Day 3: Standing on Gaia

As she kept walking down through the fields towards the beach, Ayana felt a sense of contentment well over her. The grass tickled her ankles. The earth of Sanuela seemed to pulse beneath her feet, like a living thing, reminding her of all the stories that had been spun here. She closed her eyes and felt the knowledge and the secrets of the ancestors drift in the air.

...

Please take a few moments to stand firmly and safely, and close your eyes. Breathe through your heart chakra. Feel the physical connection you have with Gaia (Mother Earth, Pachamama, ...) in this moment.

How does it feel? Safe? Gaia provides you with support. Your body is composed of her tiny particles and waves. All else that we can see, touch, hear, or smell is also formed by her. She clothes you, nourishes you, and provides you with a stable base to stand on.

You could even call her Mother Goddess Gaia if you like. That might sound overly religious, over-the-top, or whatever for some, and that's totally fine. I just call her Gaia because I want to be her friend, companion, and lover. Others refer to her as Mother Earth. Find the name that resonates most with you.

As with everything in this course, I can only show you some perspectives, and you can creatively and intuitively incorporate some of it into your life.

Can you find a moment and a way to be inwardly deeply thankful to Gaia, or whatever you call her? Breathe through your heart chakra while you do this.

Wishing you much love and looking forward to tomorrow!

Day 4: A Story of Love and Growth

She remembered tales she had heard since she was a young girl, stories about courage and self-love, of choosing between fear or love, of expectations and despondencies, and how to overcome them.

Ayana held these ancient stories close to her, allowing their wisdom to guide her. She breathed deeply, slowly, allowing herself to be enveloped by the silent knowledge around her.

. . .

Imagine if you didn't have all this stuff from television, YouTube, social media, or whatever you have watched in the last few years or decades inside of you, but instead were filled with stories about courage and self-love, of choosing between fear or love, of expectations and despondencies, and how to overcome them.

Today, do you want to read, listen to, or watch a story that can inspire your inner growth? To intensify the experience, breathe through your heart chakra, meanwhile. That is one way of showing yourself some self-love.

With much love, I'll catch you tomorrow!

Day 5: The Whispering Wind

Do you want to balance your inner growth and healing? Then, all what you need to do is: breath more often through your heart chakra.

Surely you have noticed, that the Heart Chakra Breathing is an essential part of every day's little exercise.

How about you start breathing with your heart centre already while you read the chapter of the day? It can quickly become a very good habit that expands to more occasions.

...

As she opened her eyes, she felt a deep serenity and the knowing that she was a part of something much larger than herself. She was aware that her life was one small part of the ancient landscape of Sanuela, and it filled her heart with a sense of joy and purpose. She smiled, feeling a connection to something greater, something timeless and eternal.

This morning, she was also feeling something different. It was as if the land was calling out to her. She could feel a stirring tingle in her heart, a sense of destiny enticing her. She knew something was coming, she could feel it in her body.

The gust of wind blowing around Ayana seemed almost like a whisper, calling to her. She closed her eyes and listened intently, and soon she could make out the words: "Priestess… Ayana."

…

Take a moment for yourself. Feel yourself as part of something much larger than yourself, something that is timeless and eternal.

Breathe through your heart chakra.

Can you hear Gaia calling out to you?

What would the wind whisper in your ear?

Would you write it in your journal of love and miracles?

Until tomorrow, much love to you!

Day 6: My Light and my Love

"Greetings Ayana, my light and my love," the being spoke in her mind with a soft and warm energy. "I am Ignisia, the fire fairy butterfly, spirit, and keeper of the flames."

...

For an immediate advance in self-love, try this: Breathe through your heart chakra, and say your name out loud, followed by: "my light and my love".

Allow the words to resonate in your being, understanding the meaning when you speak or whisper them to yourself. It is one more way of gifting yourself the self-love that you deserve.

When you recognize yourself as light and love, you can appreciate all of your inner beauty, all the possibilities and completeness of who you truly are.

Love you! Until we meet tomorrow!

Day 7: An Honest Embrace

It was the kind of embrace that offered honesty, understanding, and guidance and asked nothing of her in return. The energy made her feel safe and accepted, like she could be her most honest self without judgement.

...

Although here, the "embrace" is only metaphorically used in the story of Ayana, for today's love exercise, why don't you find someone to embrace for a whole minute or two? Or, be brave and say: nine minutes!

Breathe through your heart chakra. Feel the honesty, understanding, and guidance between each other. Feel safe and accepted. Be your most honest self without judgement.

Could you describe in your journal of love and miracles what you felt during the hug?

May you feel loved, and see you tomorrow!

Day 8: Our Spirit Guides

The butterfly's voice washed over her, reminding her of what she knew in her heart: "Don't be afraid of becoming your highest light and deepest love. Trust and follow. In freeing yourself, you will free the others. Mother Goddess Sanuela has sent me to be your companion on your journey. I am here to guide you. I will light your way and keep you safe. Are you ready?"

(...)

"Listen closely," Ignisia answered, her wings fluttering in the air. "You and I are connected by something much greater than either of us can fully understand. Are you willing to learn, and ready to open your heart much wider than you have experienced before? I can impart to you the knowledge you need on your path, if you are ready and willing to accept it."

...

In the story, Ayana finds an easy connection through the fire fairy butterfly that she is seeing and hearing in her physical world.

Yet, how would it be if you could find an inner voice inside of you, "your companion on your journey", a voice that safely guides you through all your inner growth and healing challenges? Or even two of them, one with more feminine and one with more masculine energies.

We often use the phrase "Higher Self", but rarely acknowledge the two spirit guides that accompany us throughout this incarnation from start to finish, every single moment. To me, it's like a family of love. They support us while we are here in the physical body, and vice versa in other incarnations.

I have got to know my spirit guides quite well in the past few years. Before, I never even considered that this kind of contact could be possible, until they symbolically knocked on my door. So, I understand and don't mind if you're not into today's "exercise".

But if you believe this perspective could be helpful and beneficial, why not give it a try and address your spirit guides: "Dear guides, angels, elemental fairies, or spirit animals: Can we come into closer contact with each other? May I encounter you in my dreams or in my life adventures?"

Breathe through your heart chakra while you ask.

Observe what happens over the coming days! Keep inquiring. When you're ready, and when you can embrace love and not give in to fear, they may make themselves known.

Day 9: You Are Chosen

"You have been chosen, Ayana," said Ignisa. "You will be able to experience and expand your love beyond ordinary means."

...

Today, I want to thank you for reading this, for attempting the exercises, and for introducing more love into your life.

Every breath you take with love has a direct and positive influence on your environment, as well as yourself.

If you give yourself more and more moments of Heart Chakra Breathing, allowing yourself to be in love with your innermost self, you will raise your frequencies, cleanse your aura, attract new possibilities, and heal the energetic and spiritual world from egocentrism and fears.

Just breathe love in and out. Experience and expand your love beyond ordinary means.

Fasting Together: Harmonising Hearts in the Light

Would you like to be part of an online circle (think of a sacred campfire space) for safely sharing your stories and emotions, for being vulnerable and lovingly connected to others?

Would you like to combine this with one day of fasting per week, either with fruits or just water or tea?

Whether for physical or energetic health, for more light, inner self-acceptance, more openness or more awareness: Together, we can more easily build healthy routines and support ourselves in our experiences, difficulties and energetic and emotional purification processes.

I will keep reminding everyone to keep breathing through the heart chakra. This way, we speak and write from the heart and we listen and read from the heart.

There is a new topic or theme every week. You can reserve your spot here, on my website:

https://www.sensual-energetic-healing.com/fasting-together/

The exchange for the circle is what you freely want to give from your heart.

Day 10: The Inner Critic

She thought in her head: "What? Me? I'm not a High Priestess. No, I can't do this. I'm not able to give the amount of love to other people, I'm still struggling with my own self-love sometimes."

...

Do you ever notice this voice in your life, coming from your inner critic who doubts your own true greatness?

Let's give this inner critic a name so that we can talk to it more easily. Give it a size and an outfit, maybe make it an upset teenage child? After all, this voice shouldn't be too harsh on you!

Breathe through your heart chakra. Attempt to befriend your inner critic. Provide it with safety and comfort from your heart. Perhaps inquire why it wishes to keep you so small. Engage in an internal dialogue, be courageous, be compassionate.

If you like, write something in your journal.

Day 11: Your Choices

"Don't be afraid, it is a grand journey, and also an immense honour. Ayana, understand the magnitude of the task ahead of you. It is not undertaken lightly. You have been chosen by the loving goddess of Sanuela, but it is only your future to become a High Priestess if you also choose so yourself."

...

There are prophecies from your own future within you because we all strive towards becoming the fullest expression of light and love. Your deepest inner knowing, your intuition, your spirit guides – they will all bring you ever closer to your inner core of light and love.

It is up to us to choose to follow what we feel is the right path, time and again.

Do you continue to follow your path to your innermost light and love every day? Please breathe through your heart chakra, and write into your journal of love and miracles which step(s) you will take today.

Day 12: Two Questions

"What would I have to do? What if I don't succeed?"

…

These are two excellent questions for you to answer in one or more pages of your journal of love and miracles, while breathing through your heart chakra.

Question 1: What would you need to do? How could you describe your journey towards more light and more love? What steps would be calling out to you?

Question 2: What if you don't follow? Often, one's goal is not a particular achievement, but more of a directional choice. Sometimes, we hold ourselves back because we are anxious about our possible future. Gaining clarity about our personal path and various different possibilities can be a good help.

Day 13: Walking Through Fears

"*You need to learn how to balance and safely ground your love, openness, and possibilities. Make wise decisions when you are a High Priestess.*"

"*I'm still nervous, I don't know if I can manage this.*"

"*It is only natural to feel afraid. Yet, you have a strength within you that few else possess. Believe in yourself, in your light, your love, and your abilities to shine brightly from within. Your inner strength will guide you through it.*"

"*I trust in myself, but it's hard to accept what's expected from me.*"

"*That's fine. You don't have to do all the inner work at once. Take your time, make small steps along the way until you are ready for the bigger ones. You can do this, Ayana.*"

...

Our fears are our greatest inner manipulators and also our greatest opportunities for growth and inner healing. When we walk through our fears, with Heart Chakra Breathing, inner processing, or sharing with other trusted souls, we can open our hearts so much more!

When we come into inner balance and safe ground, we can release our fears, they become obsolet and fly away like shadows, making us lighter, more loving, and more free.

Take your time, make small steps along the way until you are ready for the bigger ones. You can do this.

Would you like to write about your fears in your journal today?

Until tomorrow, sending all my love!

Day 14: Our Inner Prophecy

Ayana struggled with her thoughts, as her heart pulled towards the possibility of unlocking secrets of her inner prophecy which had been hidden away until recently, however, fear of the unknown prevented her from making the leap.

She began to ponder both sides of the coin, considering the potential uncertainties and inner growth possibilities of her decision. It was true, a few moons ago in some sacred ceremonies with the elders, she had seen visions of herself as a High Priestess, but also had doubts about her courage and faith within. Now, she began to comprehend the gravity of her inner prophecy and the power of her choice.

...

We all have this inner prophecy stored within us, it is our personal storybook of consciousness and love evolution. It cannot be deleted, copied, or compared to anyone else's. This inner prophecy will always guide you.

Some of us may remember fragments of this story; it helps to guide our choices toward the best route for our inner path of growth and healing.

Maybe you remember fragments of your future self in your dreams? Or perhaps you can feel it within when something or someone is calling for you?

Discover your inner prophecy, and if you wish, write one or more versions into your journal while you breathe through your heart chakra.

Love and hugs until we meet again tomorrow!

Day 15: Releasing Emotions

Ayana breathed in, feeling the air fill her lungs. As she exhaled with a gentle release, the nervousness in her body ebbed away and became a fine astral tingling instead. The moment of calmness brought a smile to her lips.

...

This is a straightforward breathing technique that can be used to release any emotion that you have paid attention to for a few moments.

Why don't you give it a try right now? Draw in a breath from the heart chakra, letting love flow into every cell of your body. Then, as you exhale, release whatever needs to be let go.

With love, I'll be seeing you tomorrow!

Day 16: Following Our Path

Her heart was pounding with excitement as she envisaged the path of growth and inner healing that lay before her. "I'm ready", Ayana whispered confidently, with a new-found courage and resolution in her voice because she knew when to trust her inner feelings.

Ignisia flew a large curvy figure-eight before Ayana's eyes. "You have made a wise choice, Ayana. I am proud of you for trusting in the growth and love and inner healing of yourself and others."

...

Do you know this feeling, when you are initially nervous about a decision or an important step to take, and then once you are on your way, it feels totally right and good?

Then you usually know that you have chosen the correct path.

Remember, and if you wish, write a few lines about the many times when you followed your inner path, and it was the right choice.

Which decisions are there for you to take today, during this week or month?

Looking forward to tomorrow, with much love!

Day 17: Connecting with Animals

At a very young age, Ayana developed a special connection with the animals of Sanuela. She could feel their presence and energies around her, and often felt like they were speaking to her.

...

Children often still maintain a very natural inner connection with animals. Some appear to be able to sense and intuitively comprehend the emotional state of an animal quite well. Others are like an energetic magnet, attracting animals to them. And then there are some who occasionally even see the world from an animal's perspective.

These kinds of phenomena can become quite normal once you explore your capabilities to connect with animal beings around you.

For today's little exercise, why don't you find a place (in nature?) where you can connect with some animals, of any type or size. Perhaps it's a bird in a bush in front of the bus station, a cat lounging in a garden, or a dog in the park.

Simply stand or sit there for a while, tune in, and feel the animal. Let your mind go blank now; all problems and worries can wait for a moment so that you are ready to observe what wants to reveal itself on your inner canvas.

If nothing appears, don't worry. Just keep tuning in, more and more frequently. Eventually, you may notice something.

Wishing you love and until we meet again tomorrow!

Day 18: Magical Artefacts

To always remind herself of this first inner contact in the woods, she took a small stone she found next to her feet. At home, she would use this stone, holding it to reconnect with the deer whenever she felt like it.

...

Do you ever take a stone, a piece of wood, a feather, or some other object as a reminder of the energies from a certain place? These can be powerful astral artefacts if you offer them your appreciation and love.

If you wish to connect with a certain energy, simply take an object in your hand, breathe through your heart chakra, and sense it.

Would you like to seek a piece in nature today, hold it in your hands for a while and commune?

Sending you love and counting down to tomorrow!

Day 19: Telepathic Bonds

The telepathic bond that Ayana had with the deer was a unique and powerful experience for her. Often, she was capable of feeling the deer's thoughts and emotions, feeling as if they were communicating in a language that only they comprehended.

...

With animals or humans whom we love, we can experience an inner telepathic bond. As we become accustomed to this, we may not be wondering any more why someone shows up or calls after we had just been thinking about them.

Take a few breaths through your heart chakra, feel your love inside, and spend a few minutes feeling into your connection to the souls you are close with. Maybe your mind and heart want to linger a little longer with some of them? Perhaps something arises that you would like to forgive?

Think of those you haven't heard from in a while. Send them your loving energies. See what happens – who knows, they might just give you a call or send you a message, or you could meet them at an unexpected place. Of course, that would always be completely coincidental, right? ;-)

Tomorrow can't come soon enough, much love!

Day 20: Curious and Imaginative

Ayana was a curious and imaginative young woman who loved to explore the unseen world around her. She was both brave and open-minded, eager to experience any new adventure that came her way.

...

How about you? Are you curious and imaginative? Do you love to explore the unseen world around you? Are you brave and open-minded, eager to experience any new adventure that comes your way?

If any of these questions triggers you, what comes up?

Breathe through your heart centre.

Do you want to try something new today? Be curious, imaginative, or open-minded – even if it's only a small gesture. Give it a go and see how it feels!

Day 21: Being the Animal

Gazing at the birds gliding in the sky, she was overwhelmed by their freedom and joy, stirring an entrancing emotion within her. She began to muse on what it would be like to fly in unison with them.

...

Take a few moments for yourself today. Close your eyes and imagine you are a bird, flying with the others in perfect harmony.

Do you feel freedom? Joy? Or something else entirely?

In case heights are not a pleasant imagination for you, find an animal that means something to you, and feel like it.

Feel and observe, while breathing through your heart centre.

Day 22: The Eternal Now

Through her deeper inner conversations with birds, Ayana learned about the importance of being present and in the moment. The birds taught her that life is meant to be lived fully and in the present, and that dwelling on the past or worrying about the future was a waste of precious time.

...

In my books, I often refer to the present moment as the Eternal Now. There is nothing but the Now. Time is merely an idea for our brains to make sense of our experience in a three-dimensional world. Time aids us with navigation, yet it does not exist.

If you believe in reincarnation, think about how all your past and future lives are happening just in this very moment of the Eternal Now.

Breathe through your heart centre and feel this Now.

Thank you.

Day 23: Connecting with the Collective

Ayana also learned about the importance of community and connection. Birds flew in flocks, and Ayana noticed that they were always looking out for one another. They taught Ayana about the importance of working together, and how strength comes from the collective.

...

Can you find a way to connect with other souls today and do something together – with love and from your heart chakra? Are you part of a group somewhere that you can acknowledge and give thanks to, perhaps by sharing something personal?

Would you like to share with others that you are doing this self-love course, with daily suggestions and challenges?

Thank you very much.

Day 24: Giving Love to a Tree Being

Ayana also adored the tree beings, and experienced wonderful moments in conversations with them. As she walked through the forest, she would often pause to touch and caress the bark of a tree being. When she felt a connection to the being before her, she would hold it or embrace it. She then felt the ancient knowledge they held, awed by their inner wisdom. She found it charming that they never had to move or journey anywhere – they simply stood still and meditated in bliss and in the present moment, always.

...

Would you find a tree today and wrap your two hands around its stem or give it a full, heartfelt hug? Breathe through your heart chakra as you do this. Feel it meditating, sharing the moment with you.

Until tomorrow, sending love and good vibes!

Day 25: Roots From Your Feet

She learned from them the importance of strong roots to feel a deep sense of connection to Sanuela and stand tall and strong. Roots spread out in a network, reaching into the earth, growing like veins that connected to one another.

...

Find a moment, when you can firmly stand on the ground, close your eyes and feel yourself. Breathe through your heart chakra, then be aware of how your feet are connected with Mother Gaia or Earth.

Imagine, there are roots growing from your feet into the ground of Gaia, all the way to her core.

Below your feet, a network of roots connects you. Feel them. Embrace them.

Thank you.

Love you lots and see you tomorrow!

Day 26: Trusting Yourself

When she started to see tree roots as a symbol of her life, she found her personal alignment in the deep connection with other loving souls. She felt her need for community and togetherness, but she also yearned for a closer relationship with someone who would fully understand and trust her, even when she wasn't always sure how to trust herself. She knew this was an inner topic still needing work.

...

Do you have someone in your life whom you can trust? Someone whom you understand?

Do you trust yourself?

Breathe through your heart centre.

What would you like to do or change today to feel more trust in yourself and others?

May your day be filled with love, until then!

Day 27: Charging a Piece of Nature

Her friend Amun sometimes went on long journeys with his father. Usually, he brought her something beautiful back, something personal that he had found, sometimes just a stone or a beautiful feather.

...

If you can, why don't you take a walk through nature today, or find a little moment in a garden, on grass or wherever you feel connected to nature.

Breathe through your heart centre. Feel. Be open.

Look around you, on the ground. Is there a piece of wood, a beautiful stone or something from this place of nature that you can take into your hands and inwardly charge it with blessings and strength-giving energies?

Would you like to gift this charged piece of nature to someone you love, cherish, or admire?

Alternately, would you prefer to take it home and display it on your table, shelf, or meditation shrine?

Until tomorrow arrives, sending all my love!

Day 28: Another Hug?

When her craving for a more sensual connection with Kofi or Amun became too intense, and neither of them were around, she would sometimes go into the woods and ask a tree being if it wanted to be hugged.

...

Of course, you don't need any craving for a more sensual connection to touch or hug a tree. Just do it because you want to feel connected, by giving and sharing your love, your energies, and the warmth of your body.

Tune in and feel the inner strength of the tree being you are holding or embracing.

Inwardly, you can thank the being afterwards for the connection. Maybe you'd like to do this more often in the future?

Counting down the hours until tomorrow, with love!

Day 29: Step by Step

Ayana found inspiration in the strength and endurance displayed by the tree beings around her. They taught her that true growth takes time, faith, and a lot of patience. They never give up, pushing through even in tough conditions.

...

Where in your life do you want to take a step forward? It's really just this – take one step. Then, perhaps tomorrow, you can take another. Just keep going, step by step.

This way, there is no need to give up, and even in tough conditions you will find a way to go one step further. That is all that is required for consistent growth towards the direction you wish to expand.

Until tomorrow, much love and warm wishes!

Day 30: Meditation Time

Meditating was of particular benefit to Ayana. She learned how to still her mind and focus her attention on the present moment and on breathing through her heart centre. Sometimes, she visualised and experienced a floating bubble of love and light surrounding her, radiating like a white sphere.

…

To be honest, I don't meditate regularly any more. I used to, at times three hours a day, when I lived in a spiritual community with other disciples of Yogananda. Now, I love to enjoy meditative states wherever I am.

You may find this simple visualisation helpful in any small moment in between, when you are waiting for someone or something, or, simply would like to savour the Eternal Now, while giving it a bit of direction and purpose.

See you tomorrow, with love and excitement!

A Couple More Days...

We are almost finished with the initial part of the course. If you would like to carry on receiving self-love activities after Day 33, I invite you to choose what you would like to give back from your heart if you haven't done this already.

It's completely up to you. Follow your intuition and give it with an open heart.

Additionally, please spread the word about this course and share it with your friends. Your support is much appreciated, and it allows me to continue writing.

If you're not receiving updates for this book automatically on your reader (e.g. Kindle), make sure to check for them regularly.

Day 31: The Mother Goddess

Ayana was taught from a young age about the loving planetary consciousness of Mother Goddess Sanuela. She learned that the planet, as a whole, was a living, conscious, and loving organism and wanted to be treated as such by her children, with care and kindness.

...

It took me a long time to truly comprehend, deep within, that we are living on a living, conscious, and loving organism. We call her Mother Earth or Gaia, yet how often do we, her children, really strive to sense her presence, her internal energetic heartbeat, her divine breath?

Our loved ones, institutions, religions, and media may have indoctrinated us with outdated and encrusted beliefs that humans were the highest form of consciousness. Unravelling these deeply rooted convictions can take time.

Mother Gaia is the source of our human existence – providing us with our bodies, clothes, nourishment, she even gives us the air to breath. Let's embrace her today by offering a symbolic gesture of gratitude.

With anticipation for tomorrow, much love to you!

Day 32: Respect and Love

The people of Sanuela were taught to treat humans, plants, animals, and the land itself with their highest respect and love, taking only what was necessary and giving back more than what was taken.

...

How do you treat humans, plants, animals, and the land itself? Do you give your highest respect and love, taking only what is necessary and giving back more than what was taken?

Today, can you find and improve one of your habits, giving more respect and love?

Until tomorrow, may you feel loved and cherished!

Day 33: I AM

The teachings Ayana received in Sanuela's learning circles showed her how Mother Goddess Sanuela was sharing parts of her vast consciousness with all her inhabitants. She emanates soul particles, forming together to bigger structures, until they perceived themselves as individual beings with an understanding of I AM.

...

When I asked my spirit guides, this is how I perceived how you and me came to our understanding of I AM, whether you are a child of Gaia or your soul originated from some distant planet. We were born in the same way, from a common source, soul particles that came together to form a bigger sense of identity.

We are not done growing yet. This sense of I AM can expand to include our whole personal universe, celebrating divine love in the Eternal Now. From this point onwards, we become goddesses and gods ourselves.

Today, take some time to meditate on this.

The Ending or Just the Beginning?

This is the end of Season 1 of the Course in Love and Miracles. I hope you have enjoyed this journey together.

Thank you for sharing your time and energies with Ayana, Sanuela, Gaia / Mother Earth, and with your inner heart centre.

Please keep staying in your heart a little more every day.

Appendix

About the Author

Born as the youngest in a family of psychologists and pedagogues, I strongly felt drawn to the more unconventional paths of learning and discovering my abilities, gifts, and passions. I quit the school system early and preferred to spend three years in the Ananda Assisi community, initiated as a disciple of Paramhansa Yogananda ("Autobiography of a Yogi") by a direct disciple, Swami Kriyananda.

After three years of community, meditation time and inner development, I followed love and adventure, and was drawn into the maelstrom of the "modern" world. I learned how to drink and party, how to become addicted to an unhealthy lifestyle, and how to become either burned out or depressed as a result. In some long relationships, I loved my partners, endured both love and suffering; experienced all which life had to offer.

I experienced business life in its various phases – ups and downs, different directions and goals – designing advertisements, logos, or websites, bringing people together, making professional videos. I also studied and practised hypnotherapy and relaxation therapy practices, producing my own library of guided imagery and audio meditations; more than 80 titles are available in German.

On the beautiful island of Tenerife, I re-connected with my spiritual needs.

While programming apps for meditation and relaxation, I consulted various shamanic guides, participated in ceremonies with and without traditional shamanic plant medicine, engaged in cleansing and transformational rituals, and attended many retreats in complete darkness.

Right at the start of The Big Change in 2020, I was contacted by my spirit guides. They knocked three times at my door, quite literally: I found small pieces of wood on three successive days in my food, and wondered how to interpret that, if this was all a half-awakened dream universe.

I found out I'm not alone. I can communicate and, more importantly, love my spirit guides. They are part of me and I feel one with them. Just like me, you also have at least two spirit guides. Until now, my guides have never given me wrong information. We trust each other and love each other.

As for my daily life, I strive to live a fairly regular life – writing a lot. I also enjoy the wonderful nature of Tenerife. A few years ago, I was gifted a sailing licence course and I adore taking pictures, meaningful conversations, creating art... But yes, my writing takes up a lot of time.

I learnt and evolved through my intuitive writing. I ask questions and receive answers that surprise me again and again, even though I know the answers are coming from the same central well of cosmic knowledge that I feel within myself. So, writing often feels like remembering to me.

I experienced and wrote about chakra healing, kundalini, astral energies, other-dimensional experiences, shamanic ceremonies, conscious and sacred sensuality, and how to work through the inner processes on the spiritual path; such as fears, emotional pains, or guilt.

For myself, I found that there is one formula that surpasses all: LOVE. When love is present, then multidimensional healing and growth follow.

Hooray, I am Human!

Sensual Energetic Healing (SEH) for Singles & Couples

For souls seeking closeness, Sensual Energetic Healing (SEH) is a beautiful meditation experience with heart and touch. Hooray, we are humans and not bio-robots! Let's learn a new coming together with each other, let´s open our heart chakras and expand our capacity to love…

For singles, SEH is an easy, new way to more human closeness. Couples can balance their togetherness, deepening and refining their connection. Or, if both agree, they look for one or more energetic healing partners to experience the meditative, loving embrace with other souls together.

We experience being held, forgiven, trusted and unconditionally loved.

We let go.

We feel ourselves.

High Priestess of Sanuela

Spiritual Fantasy Romance

"Don't be afraid of becoming your highest light and deepest love.

Trust and follow. In freeing yourself, you will free the others."

A fire fairy butterfly, spirit and keeper of the flames, offers the young woman Ayana to follow the calling of her inner prophecy to become a High Priestess of Sanuela. Will she be able to let go of her fears, develop her energetic healing abilities and take on the responsibility to create beautiful visions of love for the good of Sanuela?

Ayana, My Light and My Love

Sensual Spiritual Romance

Ayana, a High Priestess of Sanuela, brings love, blessings, and inner healing to her world. She awakens pure, unconditional love in the souls' hearts and guides their longing towards self-discovery and inner wholeness.

Guided by Goddess Sanuela and her spirit guides, she radiates her loving, astral healing energies to each visiting soul, embracing, caressing and supporting them on their path towards inner growth and healing.

Through intimate encounters of sacred sensuality, exploration of her masculine and feminine sides, and the pursuit of inner unity, Ayana navigates challenges and grows closer to fulfilling her prophecy.

This enchanting tale invites readers to embrace love, healing, and the power of unity in a new awakening world.

Other Books

Human Connection, Unconditional Love, New Relationships, and Sacred Sensuality in the World of Sanuela

Embrace a new paradigm of love, authenticity, and mutual growth in this enchanting tale of heartfelt connections and profound transformations.

Enchantress of Sensual Bliss

Isadora and Leandro attend Lana Lightweaver's sacred sensuality course in the magical lands of Sanuela - an exploration of their intimacy that leads to newfound appreciation and enhances their honesty and love with one another.

Balancing Emotional Needs: A New Relationship With Food

Struggling with food cravings, emotional eating, or feeling out of sync with your body? This book offers a path towards a new relationship with food, one guided by self-love and spiritual awareness. You'll find practical advice, relatable examples, and transformative insights that are easy to understand and apply.

Allowing LOVE

Allowing LOVE Two

Allowing LOVE Three

Each book contains 99 poems about LOVE abundance and kundalini, holy trinity and freedom, fears and shadows, allowances and boundaries, awakening and sacred sensuality, consciousness and Maria Magdalena, Yin and Yang, ... and more.

Love Beyond Jealousy

The complex emotion of jealousy can be tamed by understanding its many facets and by practising honest, loving communication, empathy, and compersion.

Blog, Online Circles, and Retreats

You can find the best overview of all my projects and books on my central website www.nils-klippstein.de/en.

How Do You Feel About the Book?

Thank you for your choice in picking this book. May it have added some value and quality to your everyday life.

If you found benefit in reading it, I'd like you to spread the word by sharing to your favorite social media accounts, so that your friends and family can also enjoy it.

Moreover, kindly consider posting a review for me. Your comments and encouragements will help me as an author for future projects, and will be highly appreciated.

Thank you!

www.ingramcontent.com/pod-product-compliance
Lightning Source LLC
Chambersburg PA
CBHW022000170726
47994CB00021B/1345